I0575742

LaDainian Tomlinson

by Michael Sandler

Consultant: Norries Wilson
Head Football Coach, Columbia University

New York, New York

Credits

Cover, © Mike Blake/Reuters/Landov; Title Page, © Elsa/Getty Images; 4, Courtesy of Jesse Arroyo/San Diego Chargers; 5, © Sean M. Haffey/Union-Tribune via Getty Images; 6, © AP Images/Denis Poroy; 7, © AP Images/Denis Poroy; 8, © Sylvia Allen/NFL/Getty Images; 9, © AP Images/Campbell's Chunky Soup, Fred Greaves; 10, © Brian Bahr/Allsport/Getty Images; 11, © David Bergman/Icon SMI/Newscom; 12, © Icon SMI/Newscom; 13, © Tracy Frankel/NFL/Getty Images; 14, © Peter Read Miller/Sports Illustrated/Getty Images; 15, © AP Images/Denis Poroy; 16, Courtesy ladainiantomlinson.com; 17, © Eddie Perlas Photography; 18, Courtesy Mike Nowak/San Diego Chargers; 19, © Sarah Borth/Waco Tribune; 20, © AP Images/Denis Poroy; 21, © Ben Liebenberg/Newscom; 22, © Elsa/Getty Images; 22Logo, © KRT/Newscom.

Publisher: Kenn Goin
Senior Editor: Lisa Wiseman
Creative Director: Spencer Brinker
Photo Researcher: Nancy Tobin
Design: Dawn Beard Creative

Library of Congress Cataloging-in-Publication Data

Sandler, Michael, 1965–
LaDainian Tomlinson / by Michael Sandler ; consultant: Norries Wilson.
p. cm. — (Football heroes making a difference)
Includes bibliographical references and index.
ISBN-13: 978-1-59716-774-1 (library binding)
ISBN-10: 1-59716-774-6 (library binding)
1. Tomlinson, LaDainian—Juvenile literature. 2. Football players—United States—Biography—Juvenile literature. I. Wilson, Norries. II. Title.

GV939.T65S37 2009
796.332092—dc22
[B]

2008032806

For more information, write to Bearport Publishing Company, Inc., 101 Fifth Avenue, Suite 6R, New York, New York 10003. Printed in the United States of America.

10 9 8 7 6 5 4 3 2 1

CONTENTS

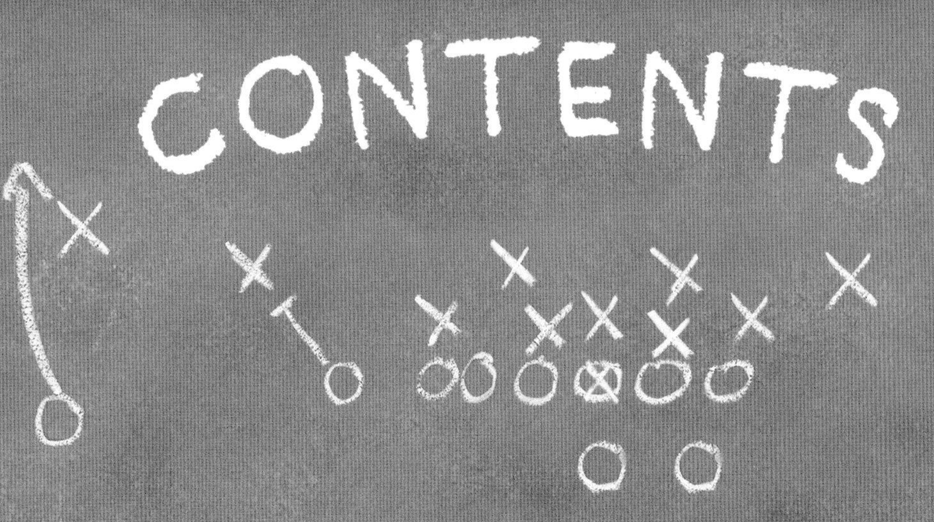

The Magic Moment

"LT! LT! LT!" the crowd chanted. The San Diego Chargers' stadium was full of fans screaming for star **running back** LaDainian Tomlinson (LT). They knew that he was about to break the **NFL** single-season touchdown record.

Then came the **snap**. The Chargers' quarterback Philip Rivers handed LT the ball. The 5' 10" (1.77 m) **rusher** ran to his left. LT blew by Denver Broncos **cornerback** Darrent Williams and rolled into the **end zone**. Touchdown!

The stadium erupted. LT hadn't only scored. He had run right into the record book.

Fans cheering on LT

LT (#21) scored his record-breaking touchdown against the Denver Broncos on December 10, 2006.

LT's touchdown not only broke the NFL single-season record, it was also his 29th of the year.

Team Player

After the game, the fans shouted "LT! **MVP**!" Reporters crowded around the San Diego players to ask questions about the running back. Everyone was talking about LaDainian—everyone but LT.

LT was a team player. As soon as he scored the touchdown, he was thinking about his teammates. Breaking the record was something for every Charger to share.

"When we're old, we'll be able to tell our kids, tell our grandchildren," said LT. "We can talk about something special that we did. *We* made history today."

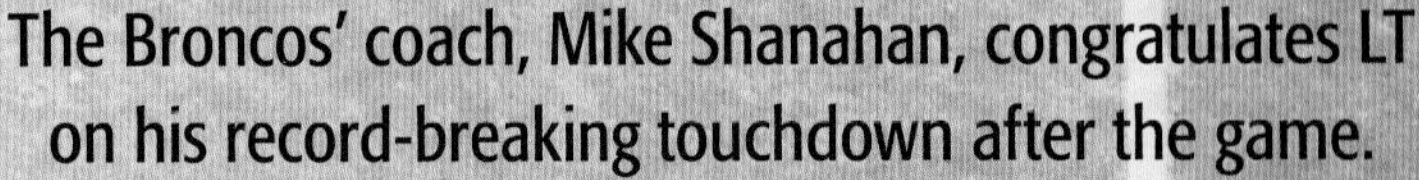

The Broncos' coach, Mike Shanahan, congratulates LT on his record-breaking touchdown after the game.

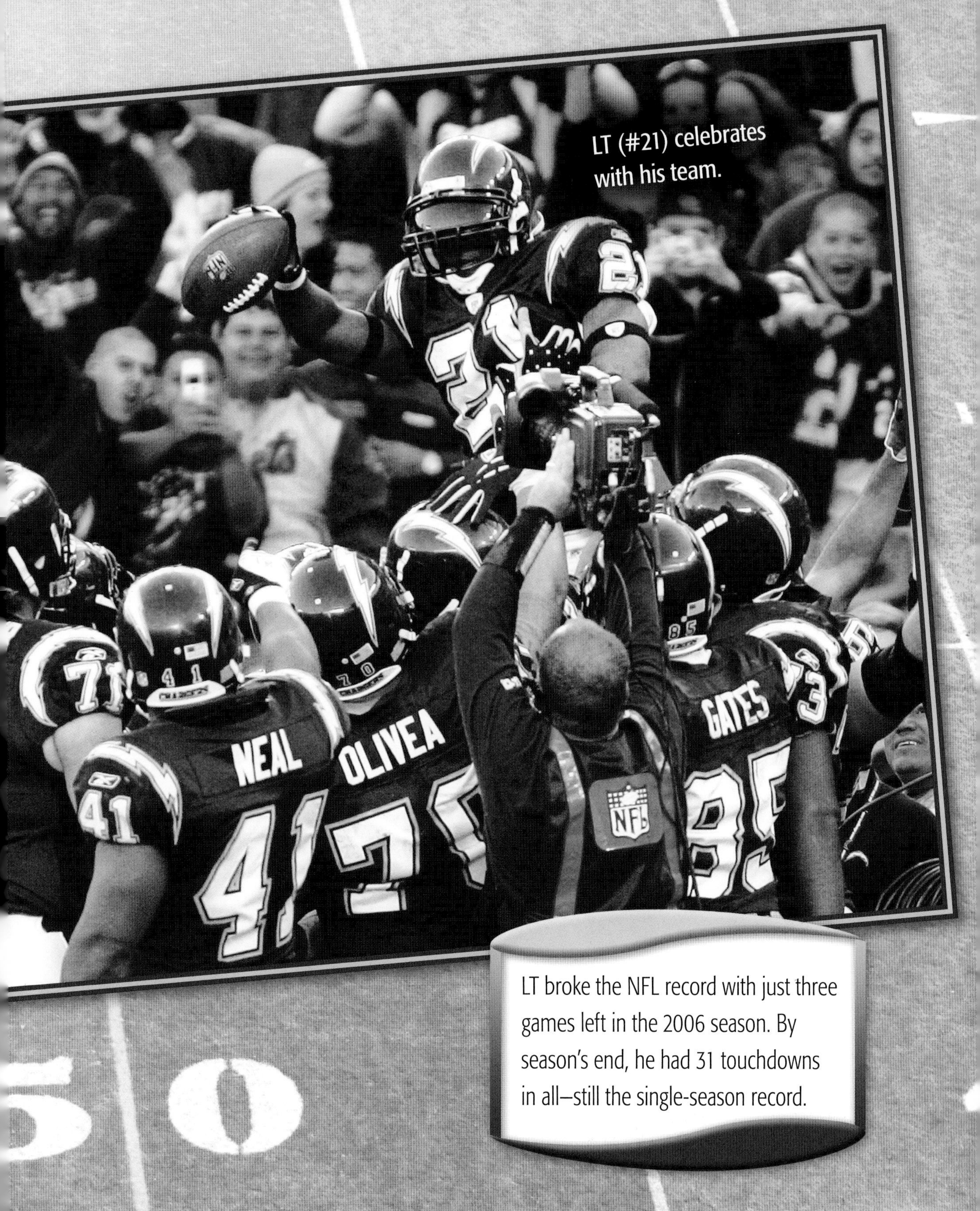

LT (#21) celebrates with his team.

LT broke the NFL record with just three games left in the 2006 season. By season's end, he had 31 touchdowns in all—still the single-season record.

Growing Up in Texas

Thinking about others first wasn't new for LT. Growing up in Waco, Texas, he always worried about his family. He tried to help his mom—a single parent struggling to raise three kids—with the dishes and other chores. "LaDainian did what he thought would keep us happy," she remembers.

What made LT happy was football. He simply loved the sport. LaDainian watched it on TV. He played every chance he could. He even went to sleep cradling a football in his arms.

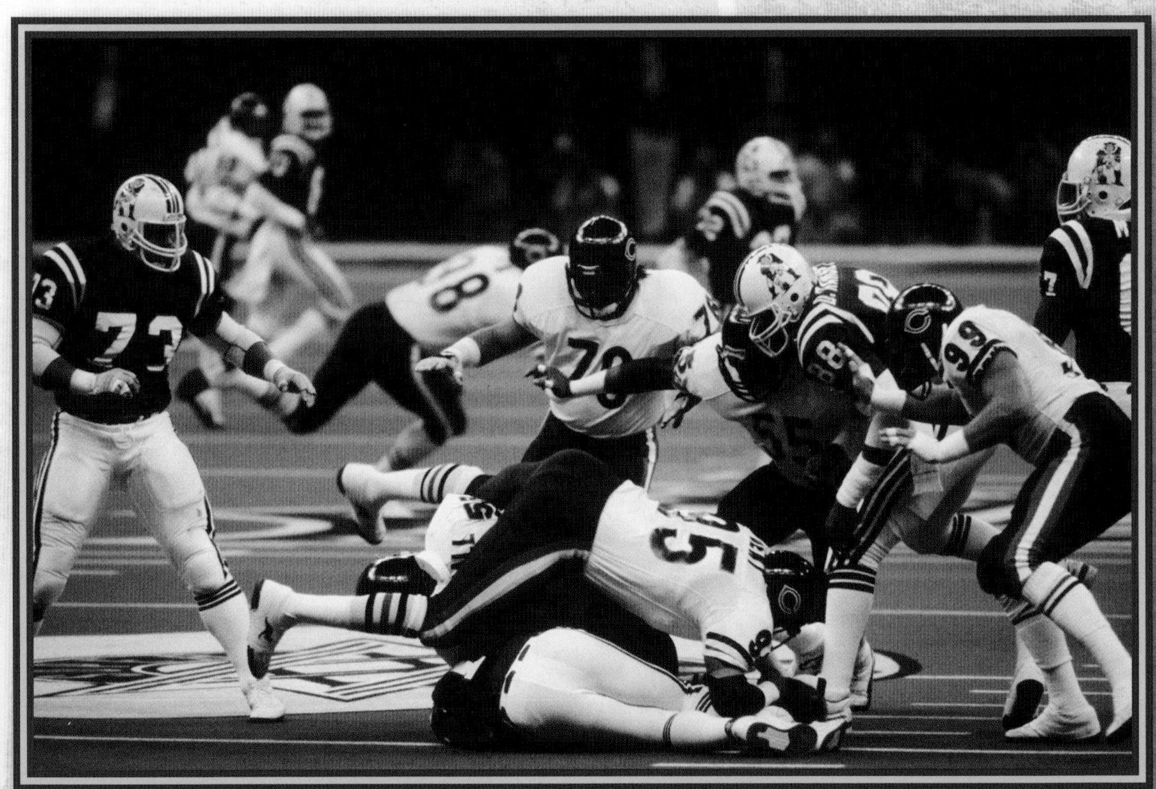

Growing up, LT enjoyed watching the Chicago Bears play on TV.

LT and his mom

When LT was eight years old, he wrote a letter to his mother. In it, he promised that one day he would buy her a big, new house. LT kept his promise, and today his mom lives in a big, new house.

Super Rusher

LT's childhood **idols** were two running backs—the Dallas Cowboys' Emmitt Smith and the Chicago Bears' Walter Payton. He always tried to copy their moves—with a lot of success.

By high school, LT was a star. Many different colleges hoped he would come and play for them. Eventually, LaDainian chose Texas Christian University (TCU).

By his junior year, the powerful yet graceful running back was the nation's leading rusher. In one game alone, he gained an incredible 406 yards (371 m). Naturally, NFL teams were eager to sign him. In 2001, LT was **drafted** by the San Diego Chargers.

The great Emmitt Smith (#22), one of LT's idols

LT holds up his Chargers jersey on draft day in 2001.

LT was the fifth player chosen in the 2001 draft.

San Diego Star

LaDainian became a **starter** right out of training camp. Soon he was wowing everyone with his skills. LT ran right over defenders. He could hold on to passes just as well as the league's best **receivers**. He was so good he made the **Pro Bowl** after his second season.

Sadly, LT had little help from his teammates during his first years in San Diego. The Chargers lost a lot more games than they won. LT could have left to play for a better team. Instead, he just worked harder. Sooner or later, he felt, the team would turn around.

LT stretches to make a catch during a game against the New York Jets in 2002.

LT has thrown seven touchdown passes in his career.

LT doesn't just run and catch. On some plays, he also throws the ball like a quarterback.

Breaking Through

The turnaround for the Chargers came in 2004. San Diego rolled to a 12-4 record. They won the **AFC** West and made it to the playoffs for the first time in nine years. Then, in 2006, LaDainian had the kind of year players spend all their lives dreaming about.

LT broke NFL records for touchdowns, points, and multi-touchdown games. He was named league MVP and NFL Man of the Year. No football star shined brighter. Around the country, kids looked up to LT the same way he had admired Walter Payton and Emmitt Smith as a child.

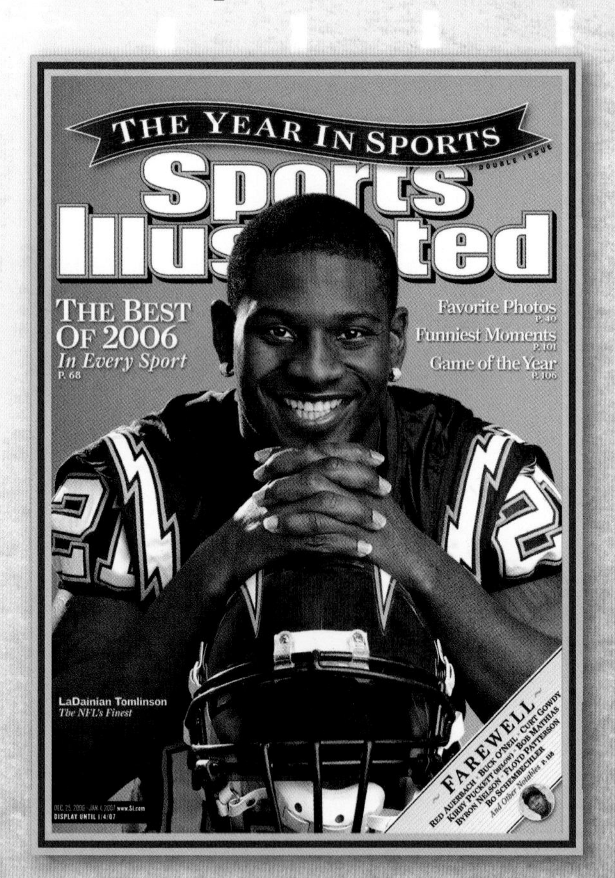

In 2006, San Diego won 14 games and lost only 2. It was the best record in the team's history.

LT (#21) jumps over a St. Louis Rams linebacker during a game in 2006.

Role Model

LT has never forgotten what it's like to look up to an athlete. He remembers a special moment when he was 13 years old. At football camp, he got to meet one of his idols, Emmitt Smith. During a **drill**, Emmitt himself handed LT the ball. "I kind of took it as a sign of things to come," LT remembers.

Today, LT tries to be for others what Emmitt is to him—a hero. That's why he started the Touching Lives **Foundation**. This group's goal is to **enhance** the lives of less fortunate children and families through various activities. For example, the foundation **sponsors** LT's 21 Club, which gives children the chance to go to a Chargers home game. LT buys the tickets and then spends time with the kids on the field after the game.

Each summer, LT runs football camps for kids in Waco, Texas; Fort Worth, Texas; and San Diego, California.

LT poses with some kids from the 21 Club. They not only get to go to a game, they also receive a bag filled with books, school supplies, and games.

Why is the club called "21"? It's LT's jersey number.

Touching Lives

Through his foundation, LT reaches out to people in many ways. On Thanksgiving, for example, he buys turkey dinners for about 2,000 needy San Diego families. Then at Christmastime, he visits hospitals, cheering up sick kids and giving away toys. "They're so grateful to be getting toys," says LT. "You can't help but enjoy yourself."

The Touching Lives Foundation also sponsors the "LT School is Cool" program. Each year it provides 30 kids from San Diego and Waco with $1,000 college **scholarships**.

LT visiting a young boy in the hospital

LT and LaTorsha (center) surrounded by the 2008 "School is Cool" scholarship award winners

LT runs the Touching Lives Foundation with his wife, LaTorsha.

Most Important

In January 2008, LT led San Diego to the **AFC Championship Game** against the New England Patriots. Sadly, he hurt his knee on the very first play. Without their star, the Chargers lost the game and a chance to go to the Super Bowl.

LT was disappointed, but he didn't get upset. He knows some things are more important than winning football games.

"People may remember something I did on the field for a couple of days, maybe a week," he says. "But the things that I do and we do in the community are something that people remember for the rest of their lives."

LT sits on the sidelines during a playoff loss to the New England Patriots.

LT spends time with some of his fans.

LT has rushed for over 10,000 yards (9,144 m) in seven seasons with San Diego.

The LT File

LaDainian is a football hero on and off the field. Here are some highlights.

- LT started playing league football in first grade. On the very first snap of his very first game, he ran all the way for a touchdown.
- How does LT have the energy to gain all those yards? By eating lots of his favorite foods: turkey, collard greens, and macaroni and cheese.
- LT led the Chargers into the playoffs in 2004, 2006, and 2007. He has also been chosen for the Pro Bowl five times.
- After Chargers games, LT used to take all the 21 Club kids out to dinner. He had to stop because he attracted too much attention—and all the kids fought to sit next to him.
- In 2007, LT moved up to third place on the NFL's list of running backs who have scored the most touchdowns, just ahead of his idol Walter Payton.

Glossary

AFC (AY-EFF-SEE) the American Football Conference; one of two conferences in the NFL

AFC Championship Game (AY-EFF-SEE CHAM-pee-uhn-*ship* GAME) a playoff game that determines which AFC team will go to the Super Bowl

cornerback (KOR-nur-bak) a player on defense who usually covers the other team's receivers

drafted (DRAFT-id) picked after college to play for an NFL team

drill (DRIL) a training exercise used to make players better

end zone (END ZOHN) the area at either end of a football field where touchdowns are scored

enhance (en-HANSS) to make something better or greater

foundation (foun-DAY-shuhn) an organization that supports or gives money to worthwhile causes

idols (EYE-duhlz) heroes; people whom others look up to and respect

MVP (EM-VEE-PEE) the most valuable player in a game or season

NFL (EN-EFF-ELL) short for National Football League

Pro Bowl (PROH BOHL) the yearly all-star game for the season's best NFL players

receivers (ri-SEE-vurz) players who catch passes

running back (RUHN-ing BAK) a player who carries the ball on running plays

rusher (RUHSH-ur) a player whose job it is to run with the football

scholarships (SKOL-ur-ships) awards that help pay for people to go to college

snap (SNAP) the passing of the ball from the center to the quarterback, which puts the football into play

sponsors (SPON-surz) supports people who are doing something worthwhile, such as charity work

starter (START-ur) a person who plays at the start of a game; the best player at a position

Bibliography

CBS News. *60 Minutes*. "L.T.: Off-Field Work Is More Important" (December 9, 2007).

Keith, Ted. "Mr. Nice Guy." *Sports Illustrated Kids* (December 2006/January 2007).

Van Meter, David. "In the Running." *TCU Magazine* (January 2000).

Chargers.com

www.ladainiantomlinson.com

Read More

Ellenport, Craig. *LaDainian Tomlinson: All-Pro On and Off the Field*. Berkeley Heights, NJ: Enslow (2007).

Gigliotti, Jim. *LaDainian Tomlinson*. Mankato, MN: Child's World (2008).

Schmalzbauer, Adam. *The History of the San Diego Chargers*. Mankato, MN: Creative Education (2005).

Learn More Online

To learn more about LaDainian Tomlinson, the Touching Lives Foundation, and the San Diego Chargers, visit **www.bearportpublishing.com/FootballHeroes**

Index